Wok Cookbook

77 Recipes to Prepare at Home. Thai, Chinese and Indian Wok Dishes

By

G000037627

Adele Tyler

The trademarks that are used are without any consent, and the publication of the trademark is without permission or backing by the trademark owner. All trademarks and brands within this book are for clarifying purposes only and are owned by the owners themselves, not affiliated with this document.

Table of contents

INTRODUCTION 8

CHAPTER 1: WELCOME TO THE WORLD OF WOK
BREAKFAST RECIPES 10

1.1 Wok Chinese Breakfast Recipes 10

1.2 Wok Thai Breakfast Recipes 15

1.3 Wok Indian Breakfast Recipes..21

CHAPTER 2: WOK LUNCH RECIPES.................................27

2.1 Wok Chinese Lunch recipes...27

2.2 Wok Thai Lunch Recipes..33

2.3 Wok Indian Lunch Recipes 40

CHAPTER 3: WOK DINNER RECIPES 47

3.1 Wok Chinese Dinner Recipes 47

3.2 Wok Thai Dinner Recipes 53

3.3 Wok Indian Dinner Recipes...59

CHAPTER 4: WOK SNACK RECIPES 65

4.1 Wok Chinese Snack Recipes..65

4.2 Wok Thai Snack Recipes..69

4.3 Wok Indian Snack Recipes 72

CHAPTER 5: WOK VEGETARIAN RECIPES 77

5.1 Wok Chinese Vegetarian Recipes..77

5.2 Wok Thai Vegetarian Recipes..82

5.3 Wok Indian Vegetarian Recipes 90

CONCLUSION 99

Introduction

Wok as a cooking utensil has been considered to be first created and used in China, more than 2000 years in the era of the Han tradition. The name Wok has been extracted from the Cantonese word signifying "Cooking Pot", the early models of the wok were made of cast iron metals, permitting them to be more solid and enduring.

A wok is characterized as a round lined cooking utensil with high sides, generally planned with two side handles or one bigger handle. The round lower part of a wok takes into account warmth to be conveyed more equally than a pan, which means food can be prepared in a less measure of time. The high walls allow the food to be tossed easily, such as when cooking a stir fry, meaning all the things can be mixed and cooked evenly throughout.

Food specialists have various speculations with respect to why the wok was developed.

Some state that because of the deficiency of food back in the Han tradition, the wok took into consideration a wide assortment of suppers to be cooked utilizing similar fixings because of its adaptability. There is also a theory that due to different clans travelling across the country many years ago and having to carry all their belongings with them, they needed a utensil that was not only portable but also able to quickly cook large amounts of food to feed the clan.

A third hypothesis is that because of the lack of fuel and oil in the Han line, the wok took into account individuals to prepare dinners utilizing next to no oil. You will learn from the different recipes in the book below that you possibly need a limited quantity of vegetable oil when utilizing a wok at home to cook your meals.

Nowadays, the wok is utilized everywhere in the world for an entire scope of various meals. Most of the woks are produced using carbon steel, which makes it light weight and easy to use. Obviously, preparing Asian food depends intensely on the wok, yet there are so numerous different uses for the wok.

In this book, you will learn various recipes of three different nations namely the Thai, Chinese and Indian Nations. The recipe section will include breakfast, lunch, dinner, snacks, sweet dishes and not to forget the vegetarian recipes. All these recipes have been detailed with easy-to-follow instructions and detailed ingredients that will help you out in cooking by yourself at home.

Chapter 1: Welcome to the World of Wok Breakfast Recipes

If you currently do not have a wok, getting one is our recommendation. Its extraordinary apt shape functions admirably for scrambling eggs, and many other breakfast dishes. Following are some amazing breakfast Thai, Chinese, and Indian recipes that you can follow by using a wok:

1.1 Wok Chinese Breakfast Recipes

- **Wok Chinese Stir Fried Eggs with Mushrooms and Zucchini**

Preparation time: 25 minutes

Cooking Time: 15 minutes

Serving: 4

Ingredients:

- Asian Sesame oil, two tbsp.

- Chopped garlic, two tsp.
- Green onions, three tbsp.
- Bell pepper strips, half cup
- Zucchini, two cups
- Chopped fresh dill, two tbsp.
- Vegetable oil, two tbsp.
- Soy sauce, two tbsp.
- Salt to taste
- Black pepper to taste
- Mushrooms, two cups
- Eggs, six
- Chopped onions, two tbsp.

Instructions:

1. Heat a wok.
2. In a bowl, whisk together eggs, soy sauce, sesame oil, salt and pepper.
3. Add vegetable oil and swirl to coat pan.
4. Add onion and garlic and mix well.
5. Add mushrooms and mix well.
6. Spread into a single layer and cook, undisturbed, for thirty seconds.
7. Add zucchini and red pepper and mix well.
8. Cook, tossing often, until mushrooms are tender and zucchini and pepper are tender-crisp, one to two minutes more.
9. Push vegetables aside.

10. Stir in egg mixture and swirl gently to spread around pan.

11. Gently but quickly stir and mix to scramble eggs.

12. Mix vegetables into eggs as you scramble them, tossing more quickly when they are almost done.

13. When eggs are just cooked, but not dry, remove from heat.

14. Add green onions, dill and mix well.

15. Dish out your meal.

16. Your dish is ready to be served.

- **Wok Chinese Omelette**

Preparation time: 20 minutes

Cooking Time: 15 minutes

Serving: 2

Ingredients:

- Kohlrabi, one cup
- Ginger, one slice
- Soy sauce, one tbsp.
- Oil, one tbsp.
- Crab rolls, five
- Mushrooms, two
- Onions, half cup
- Rice wine, one tbsp.
- Black pepper, to taste
- Salt, to taste
- Starch, a quarter tsp.

Instructions:

1. Peel and cut the kohlrabi into thin strips.

2. Grate the onion and ginger and cut the crab rolls into rings.

3. In a Chinese wok, pour two tablespoons of oil.

4. Once hot, place the onions and ginger in.

5. Throw in the crab rolls for about half a minute, then remove the mixture from the wok and clean it with a napkin.

6. Beat the eggs with one tablespoon of water, black pepper and salt.

7. Add one tablespoon of oil to a wok, then add the well-beaten eggs.

8. On it, sprinkle the vegetables.

9. You can fold it into two or leave it as it is, then transfer it to a plate.

10. For the sauce, pour in some hot water over the mushrooms so that they swell, then drain and julienne them.

11. Blend the soya sauce, rice wine and starch.

12. Clean the Chinese wok with a napkin, pour in oil and fry the mushrooms.

13. Mix all the things together and dish out.

14. Your dish is ready to be served.

- **Wok Chinese Tomatoes and Eggs**

Preparation time: 5 minutes

Cooking Time: 5 minutes

Serving: 2

Ingredients:

- Scallions, one
- Sesame oil, two tsp.
- Vegetable oil, three tbsp.
- Sugar, two tsp.
- Medium tomatoes, four
- Eggs, four
- White pepper, a quarter tsp.
- Water, half cup

Instructions:

1. Heat the wok and add the oil.
2. Add the eggs and mix them.
3. Remove the scrambled eggs into a dish.
4. Add one more tablespoon oil to the wok, and add the tomatoes and scallions.
5. Stir-fry for one minute, and then add two teaspoons sugar, half teaspoon salt, and a quarter cup water.
6. Add the cooked eggs in the mixture.
7. Your dish is ready to be served.

- **Wok Chinese Breakfast Noodles**

Preparation time: 5 minutes

Cooking Time: 5 minutes

Serving: 2

Ingredients:

- Sesame oil, one tsp.
- Canola oil, three tbsp.
- Scallions, six
- Sugar, one tsp.
- Soy sauce, one and a half tsp.
- Ground pork, a quarter pound
- Ginger, one slice
- Dried rice noodles, one pack

Instructions:

1. Heat a wok.
2. Add canola oil around edge of wok; swirl to coat bottom and sides.
3. Add pork, half the scallions, the garlic, and ginger; cook, stirring and breaking up pork into small pieces.
4. Add soy sauce and sugar.
5. Add remaining scallions, the noodles, and sesame oil.
6. Let it cook for two minutes.
7. Your dish is ready to be served.

1.2 Wok Thai Breakfast Recipes

- **Wok Thai Spicy Pork and Eggs**

Preparation time: 10 minutes

Cooking Time: 10 minutes

Serving: 2

Ingredients:

- Ginger, one slice
- Eggs, two
- Minced pork, a quarter cup
- Shallots, half cup
- Cherry tomatoes, two
- Basil, a handful
- Cloves, six
- Sea salt, to taste
- Pepper, as required
- Vegetable oil, two tbsp.
- Caster sugar, one tsp.

Instructions:

1. Heat a large wok to a high heat and place around two tbsp. of vegetable oil in it.
2. When the oil is sizzling hot, crack an egg into it.
3. As soon as the egg touches the oil, it will begin to cook very quickly.
4. Remove most of the oil from the pan then add the ginger, garlic and chili paste and move constantly until golden brown.
5. In the afterheat of the eggs being fried this will not take long so be careful not to burn the mix.
6. Add the minced pork belly and continue to fry until the pork is crispy.

7. Add the caster sugar and cook for a further minute until the mixture darkens and caramelizes.

8. Then add the coriander, mint, basil, Thai shallots, tomatoes and fish sauce and squeeze one lime into it then toss together.

9. Your dish is ready to be served.

- **Wok Thai Noodles Stuffed Omelette**

Preparation time: 5 minutes

Cooking Time: 15 minutes

Serving Size: 4

Ingredients:

- Soy sauce, two tbsp.
- Eggs, eight
- Dried chilies, half tsp.
- Sesame oil, one tbsp.
- Cornstarch, one tsp.
- Button mushrooms, one cup
- Rice noodles, 150 grams
- Sesame seeds, one tbsp.
- White wine vinegar one tbsp.
- Green pepper, one
- Carrots, two
- Canola oil, six tbsp.
- White cabbage, one cup
- Fresh ginger, one tsp.
- Salt and pepper to taste

Instructions:

1. Mix the cornstarch with cold water in a bowl.

2. Add the eggs and whisk together until mixed.

3. Stir in the chilies and season with pepper.

4. Heat one teaspoon of the canola oil in a wok over medium heat.

5. Pour in one-quarter of the egg mixture, tipping the pan to spread out the egg in a thin, even layer.

6. Cook for two minutes or until set and golden-brown.

7. Slide the omelette out of the pan onto a plate.

8. Make three more omelettes in the same way, stacking them up interleaved with parchment paper.

9. Set aside and keep warm.

10. While making the omelettes, soak the rice noodles in boiling water to cover for four minutes, or according to the package instructions, then drain.

11. Heat the remaining two teaspoons canola oil with the sesame oil in a wok or large frying pan.

12. Add the mushrooms, carrots, pepper and cabbage and stir-fry for few minutes or until just tender.

13. Add the soy sauce, vinegar, ginger and rice noodles.

14. Gently toss together until hot.

15. Divide the vegetable and noodle mixture among the Thai omelettes and fold them over in half.

16. Sprinkle with the sesame seeds, if using, and serve immediately.

- **Wok Thai Breakfast Rice Soup**

Preparation time: 5 minutes

Cooking Time: 5 minutes

Serving Size: 4

Ingredients:

- Vegetable stock, six cups
- Sesame seeds, one tbsp.
- White rice, one cup
- Poached eggs, four
- Sautéed red cabbage, one cup
- Kimchi, half cup
- Chives, for garnish

Instructions:

1. Bring your water to a boil and add the rice in a wok.
2. Let all ingredients simmer.
3. Continue to simmer for thirty minutes until the rice soup is very creamy.
4. While the rice is simmering, you can prepare the optional garnishes.
5. Remove from heat, add your desired garnishes, and serve warm.

- **Wok Thai Style Fried Egg**

Preparation time: 15 minutes

Cooking Time: 10 minutes

Serving Size: 2

Ingredients:

- Tamarind paste, one and a half tbsp.
- Shrimps, two ounces
- Chili sauce, one tsp.
- Palm sugar, two tsp.
- Shitake mushrooms, two
- Bean sprouts, one cup
- Finely chopped shallot, one
- Eggs, four
- Oil, one tbsp.
- Sliced scallions, four
- Green onion, one
- Chopped roasted peanuts, one tbsp.
- Eggs, two
- Birds eye chili, one
- Fish sauce, two tbsp.
- Cilantro, to taste
- Butter, one tsp.

Instructions:

1. Heat the water, tamarind, fish sauce, sugar and chili until the sugar is dissolved and set aside.
2. Heat oil in a wok.
3. Add the sauce, bean sprouts, green onion and peanuts and cook for one minute.
4. Add the chili and cilantro and remove from heat and set aside.

5. Add the shrimp, shiitake, shallot and garlic and sauté for two minutes.

6. Wipe out the pan and melt the butter over medium heat.

7. Mix the eggs and the fish sauce, pour them into the pan and cook until almost set, about two minutes.

8. Spoon the shrimp mixture onto half of the omelette and fold the other half over.

9. Your dish is ready to be served.

1.3 Wok Indian Breakfast Recipes

- **Wok Indian Upma**

Preparation time: 10 minutes

Cooking Time: 15 minutes

Serving: 6

Ingredients:

- Onion, one
- Vegetable oil, one tsp.
- Sooji or semolina flour, two cups
- Ginger, two tsp.
- Tomatoes, two
- Cilantro, two tbsp.
- Water, four cups
- Salt to taste
- Mustard seeds, one tsp.
- Turmeric, half tsp.

- Chili peppers, two

- Curry leaves, two

- Coconut oil, one tsp.

- Lemon juice, one tbsp.

Instructions:

1. In a wok, roast the sooji, stirring constantly.

2. Heat the oil in the same wok.

3. Add the mustard and wait for the mustard seeds to sputter.

4. Immediately add the curry leaves, green chilies and onions.

5. Sauté until the onions are soft but not brown.

6. Add the ginger and stir in.

7. Add the turmeric and sauté another minute.

8. Add four cups water and salt.

9. Pour the roasted sooji into the wok.

10. Let it cook until fluffy.

11. Turn off the heat immediately and mix in the cilantro, lemon juice, and coconut, if using.

12. Serve in bowls with more wedges of lemon that you can squeeze over the upma.

13. Your dish is ready to be served.

- **Wok Indian Masala Oats**

Preparation time: 5 minutes

Cooking Time: 15 minutes

Serving: 2

Ingredients:

- Porridge oats, one cup
- Olive oil, one tbsp.
- Tomato, half cup
- Cumin seeds, one tsp.
- Mixed vegetables, one cup
- Chili powder, half tsp.
- Garam masala, half tsp.
- Onion, half cup
- Ginger, one inch
- Coriander leaves, for garnish
- Salt to taste

Instructions:

1. Heat olive oil in a wok.
2. Add cumin seeds.
3. When the seeds start to stove, add ginger and onions.
4. Sauté for a minute and then add the mixed vegetables.
5. For best cooking, add the tougher hard vegetables like potatoes, carrots, beans, cauliflower, and broccoli first and add the softer vegetables like bottle guard, zucchini, and pepper for two to three minutes.
6. Add tomato and all the spices.
7. Add oats and three cups of water.
8. Mix well and bring to a boil.
9. Reduce the heat to low and cook covered, with occasional stirring, until the oats are cooked and most of the water is absorbed.

10. Squeeze in the juice of a lime.

11. Garnish with coriander leaves.

12. Your dish is ready to be served.

- **Wok Indian Kagheena**

Preparation time: 15 minutes

Cooking Time: 15 minutes

Serving: 4

Ingredients:

- Tomato, one
- Eggs, six
- Butter, three tbsp.
- Cilantro, as required
- White onion, one
- Chilies, two
- Cumin seeds, one tbsp.
- Salt, as required

Instructions:

1. Break the eggs into a bowl, add salt and whisk lightly together, just enough so that the yolks combine with the whites.
2. Place a wok over a fairly medium heat, add the butter.
3. As soon as the butter stops foaming and begins to turn a nutty brown, add the onions.
4. Add the cumin seeds and fry for two minutes till aromatic.
5. Add the tomatoes and stir till warmed over and slightly soft.

6. Add cilantro, the egg mixture and chilies.

7. Continue to stir the eggs swiftly.

8. Your dish is ready to be served.

- **Wok Indian Poha Rice**

Preparation time: 10 minutes

Cooking Time: 10 minutes

Serving: 2

Ingredients:

- Turmeric, half tsp.
- Flattened rice, two cups
- Vegetable oil, two tbsp.
- Salt, as required
- Onion, half cup
- Mustard seeds, one tsp.
- Peanuts, one cup
- Green chili, two
- Curry leaves, two
- Sugar, one tsp.
- Cilantro, as required

Instructions:

1. Add flattened rice to a strainer.

2. Add turmeric and half teaspoon salt to the rice.

3. Heat oil in a wok on medium heat.

4. Once the oil is hot, add the mustard seeds and let them pop.

5. Then add the peanuts and sauté for a minute or two until they start turning brown.

6. Then add the chopped onion, green chili and curry leaves.

7. Add the green peas and cook for two minutes.

8. Then add in the rinsed rice and mix it.

9. Also add the sugar and cilantro.

10. Let it cook for two minutes.

11. Your dish is ready to be served.

Chapter 2: Wok Lunch Recipes

Meals prepared in a wok have an amazing flavor. Following are some amazing Lunch Thai, Chinese, and Indian recipes that you can follow by using a wok:

2.1 Wok Chinese Lunch recipes

- **Wok Chinese Orange Chicken**

Preparation time: 30 minutes

Cooking Time: 10 minutes

Serving: 4

Ingredients:

- Sesame oil, one tsp.
- Cornstarch, a quarter cup

- Chicken, one pound
- Dried orange peel, one tsp.
- Orange juice, a quarter cup
- Soy sauce, one tbsp.
- Garlic powder, half tsp.
- White pepper, a quarter tsp.
- Shaoxing wine, two tbsp.
- Dried chili pepper, six
- Chicken stock, a quarter cup
- Sugar, two tbsp.
- Star anise, two
- Tangerine peel, two

Instructions:

1. Mix the chicken in the sesame oil, white pepper, garlic powder, salt, and Shaoxing wine in a wok.

2. Dredge the chicken pieces in cornstarch and fry until golden.

3. Heat a wok over medium heat and add a tablespoon of oil.

4. Add the dried chili peppers, tangerine peel, and star anise, and toast for about twenty seconds, being careful not to burn the aromatics.

5. Add the orange juice, chicken stock, vinegar, sugar, and soy sauce.

6. Bring the sauce to a simmer and gradually add the cornstarch slurry, stirring constantly.

7. Mix all the things together.

8. Your dish is ready to be served.

- **Wok Chinese Black Pepper Chicken**

Preparation time: 5 minutes

Cooking Time: 25 minutes

Serving: 4

Ingredients:

- Cornstarch, a half cup
- Ginger, one slice
- Garlic, two
- Chicken, two pounds
- Black pepper, two tsp.
- Salt, to taste
- Soy sauce, two tbsp.
- Shaoxing wine, two tbsp.
- Onion, one
- Mixed vegetables, one cup
- Chopped peppers, two tsp.

Instructions:

1. Combine chicken, soy sauce, Shaoxing wine, and cornstarch in a medium-sized bowl.
2. Combine all the sauce ingredients in a small bowl.
3. Chop the aromatics and vegetables.
4. Add the onion and all the chopped peppers to another bowl.
5. Heat a tablespoon of oil in a wok.
6. Add the chicken and remove once cooked.

7. Add the remaining tablespoon of oil into the wok.

8. Add the ginger and garlic.

9. Stir the sauce mixture until the cornstarch is dissolved completely, and pour it into the wok.

10. Add all the things together and then mix in the black pepper.

11. Your dish is ready to be served.

- **Wok Chinese Chicken and Mushroom**

Preparation time: 10 minutes

Cooking Time: 5 minutes

Serving: 4

Ingredients:

- Soy sauce, two tbsp.
- Mushrooms, two cups
- Chicken, two pounds
- Vegetable oil, two tbsp.
- Cornstarch, two tbsp.
- Sesame oil, two tbsp.
- Sugar, one tsp.
- Oyster sauce, two tbsp.
- Pepper to taste
- Salt, as required
- Chinese cooking wine, two tsp.

Instructions:

1. Add the oil in a wok.

2. Add in the chicken and cook it properly.

3. Remove the chicken from the wok.

4. Next add the mushrooms and cook it.

5. Add the chicken and rest of the ingredients.

6. In the end add the cornstarch and once the dish thickens switch off the heat.

7. Your dish is ready to be served.

- **Wok Chinese Kung Pao Chicken**

Preparation Time: 10 minutes

Cooking Time: 10 minutes

Serving: 6

Ingredients:

- Soy sauce, two tbsp.
- Sugar, two tbsp.
- Chicken one pound
- Baking soda, one tsp.
- Cornstarch, one tsp.
- Chicken stock, half cup
- Hoisin sauce, one tsp.
- Chinese black vinegar, two tbsp.
- Garlic, one tbsp.
- Peanuts, half cup
- Sesame oil, two tsp.
- Sichuan pepper, one tbsp.
- Red bell pepper, one
- Green bell pepper, one

- Dried chilies, eight
- Green onions, half cup

Instructions:

1. Combine all ingredients for the chicken in a small bowl.
2. Let it rest for ten minutes approximately.
3. Whisk sauce ingredients together until sugar dissolves.
4. Add two tablespoons of cooking oil, allow to heat up, and then add marinated chicken.
5. Fry chicken for approximately four minutes while mixing, until edges are browned.
6. Stir in garlic, ginger, chili diced peppers and Sichuan peppercorns and let it cook for one minute.
7. Give the prepared sauce a mix, then pour it into the pan and bring it to a boil while stirring.
8. Once it begins to thicken slightly, add chicken back into the pan and mix all of the ingredients through the sauce until the chicken is evenly coated and sauce has thickened.
9. Stir in green onions, peanuts and sesame oil.
10. Toss well and continue to cook for a further two minutes.
11. Your dish is ready to be served.

- **Wok Chinese Beef and Broccoli**

Preparation time: 10 minutes

Cooking Time: 5 minutes

Serving: 4

Ingredients:

- Soy sauce, two tbsp.

- Broccoli, two cups
- Beef, two pounds
- Vegetable oil, two tbsp.
- Cornstarch, two tbsp.
- Sesame oil, two tbsp.
- Sugar, one tsp.
- Oyster sauce, two tbsp.
- Pepper to taste
- Salt, as required
- Chinese cooking wine, two tsp.

Instructions:

1. Add the oil in a wok.
2. Add in the beef and cook it properly.
3. Remove the beef from the wok.
4. Next add the broccoli and cook it.
5. Add the beef and rest of the ingredients.
6. In the end, add the cornstarch and once the dish thickens, switch off the heat.
7. Your dish is ready to be served.

2.2 Wok Thai Lunch Recipes

- **Wok Chicken Thai Pad**

Preparation Time: 5 minutes

Cooking Time: 25 minutes

Serving Size: 3

Ingredients:

- Coleslaw mix, one bag
- Green onions, a quarter cup
- Shredded carrots, half cup
- Honey roasted peanuts, half cup
- Oil, three tbsp.
- Rotisserie chicken, two cups
- Linguini noodles, five ounces
- Cilantro, a quarter cup
- Soy sauce, one tbsp.
- Honey, five tbsp.
- Sesame oil, three tbsp.
- Red chili flakes, two tbsp.
- Minced garlic, four

Instructions:

1. Cook linguini noodles according to package instructions.
2. Drain when finished cooking.
3. While noodles are being cooked, whisk together in a small bowl the soy sauce, honey, sesame oil, garlic and red pepper flakes.
4. Pour sauce onto drained noodles, and toss together.
5. Add shredded cabbage, shredded carrots and shredded cilantro to the noodle mixture and mix.
6. Then gently stir in half of the chopped cilantro, green onions and peanuts, reserving the other half for garnish.

7. Serve warm or cold and garnish with remaining cilantro, green onions and chopped peanuts.

8. Your dish is ready to be served.

- **Wok Thai Satay Stir Fry**

Preparation Time: 5 minutes

Cooking Time: 25 minutes

Serving Size: 3

Ingredients:

- Coleslaw mix, one bag
- Green onions, a quarter cup
- Shredded carrots, half cup
- Honey roasted peanuts, half cup
- Oil, three tbsp.
- Rotisserie chicken, two cups
- Linguini noodles, five ounces
- Cilantro, a quarter cup
- Soy sauce, one tbsp.
- Honey, five tbsp.
- Sesame oil, three tbsp.
- Red chili flakes, two tbsp.
- Minced garlic, four
- Thai satay sauce, two tbsp.

Instructions:

1. Cook linguini noodles according to the package instructions.

2. While noodles are being cooked, whisk together in a small bowl the soy sauce, honey, sesame oil, Thai satay sauce, garlic and red pepper flakes.

3. Pour sauce onto drained noodles, and toss together.

4. Add shredded cabbage, shredded carrots and shredded cilantro to noodle mixture and mix.

5. Then gently stir in half of the chopped cilantro, green onions and peanuts, reserving the other half for garnish.

6. Serve warm or cold and garnish with remaining cilantro, green onions and chopped peanuts.

7. Your dish is ready to be served.

- **Wok Shrimp Pad Thai**

Preparation Time: 5 minutes

Cooking Time: 15 minutes

Serving Size: 4

Ingredients:

- Chopped green onions, three
- Eggs, two
- Fresh bean sprouts, half cup
- Garlic cloves, three
- Oil, three tbsp.
- Shrimp, eight ounces
- Limes, two
- Red bell pepper, one
- Flat rice noodles, eight ounces
- Dry roasted peanuts, two cups

- Soy sauce, one tbsp.
- Light brown sugar, five tbsp.
- Fish sauce, three tbsp.
- Creamy peanut butter, two tbsp.
- Rice vinegar, two tbsp.
- Sirarcha hot sauce, one tbsp.

Instructions:

1. Cook noodles according to package instructions, just until tender.
2. Heat one and a half tablespoons of oil in a wok over medium-high heat.
3. Add the shrimps, garlic and bell pepper.
4. The shrimps will cook quickly, about two minutes on each side, or until pink.
5. Add a little more oil and add the beaten eggs.
6. Scramble the eggs, breaking them into small pieces with a spatula as they cook.
7. Add noodles, sauce, bean sprouts and peanuts to the pan.
8. Toss everything to combine.
9. Top with green onions, extra peanuts, cilantro and lime wedges.
10. Your dish is ready to be served.

- **Wok Prawn Pad Thai**

Preparation Time: 5 minutes

Cooking Time: 15 minutes

Serving Size: 4

Ingredients:

- Chopped green onions, three
- Eggs, two
- Fresh bean sprouts, half cup
- Garlic cloves, three
- Oil, three tbsp.
- Prawn, eight ounces
- Limes, two
- Red bell pepper, one
- Flat rice noodles, eight ounces
- Dry roasted peanuts, two cups
- Soy sauce, one tbsp.
- Light brown sugar, five tbsp.
- Fish sauce, three tbsp.
- Creamy peanut butter, two tbsp.
- Rice vinegar, two tbsp.
- Sirarcha hot sauce, one tbsp.

Instructions:

1. Mix the sauce ingredients together.
2. Heat one and a half tablespoons of oil in a wok over medium-high heat.
3. Add the prawn and bell pepper.
4. The prawns will cook quickly, about two minutes on each side, or until pink.
5. Push everything to the side of the pan.
6. Add a little more oil and add the beaten eggs.

7. Scramble the eggs, breaking them into small pieces with a spatula as they cook.

8. Add noodles, sauce, bean sprouts and peanuts to the pan.

9. Toss everything to combine.

10. Top with green onions, extra peanuts, cilantro and lime wedges.

11. Your dish is ready to be served.

- **Wok Beef and Mixed Pepper Stir Fry**

Preparation Time: 10 minutes

Cooking Time: 5 minutes

Serving: 4

Ingredients:

- Soy sauce, two tbsp.
- Mixed pepper, two tbsp.
- Beef, two pounds
- Vegetable oil, two tbsp.
- Cornstarch, two tbsp.
- Sesame oil, two tbsp.
- Sugar, one tsp.
- Oyster sauce, two tbsp.
- Pepper to taste
- Salt, as required
- Chinese cooking wine, two tsp.

Instructions:

1. Add the oil in a wok.

2. Add in the beef and cook it properly.

3. Add the beef and rest of the ingredients.

4. In the end add the cornstarch and once the dish thickens switch off the heat.

5. Your dish is ready to be served.

2.3 Wok Indian Lunch Recipes

- **Wok Indian Chicken Korma**

Preparation Time: 10 minutes

Cooking Time: 20 minutes

Serving: 2

Ingredients:

- Vegetable oil, half cup
- Ginger paste, one tsp.
- Chicken, one pound
- Garam masala, half tsp.
- Coriander powder, one tsp.
- Chili powder, one tbsp.
- Cardamom, six
- Garlic paste, one tsp.
- Yoghurt, one cup
- Salt, to taste
- Coriander, as required
- Onion, two
- Saffron, a pinch

Instructions:

1. Heat the vegetable oil into a pan.
2. Put cardamom, cloves, garlic and fry the mix properly.
3. Then add the chicken and let it cook for about two minutes.
4. Keep stirring it.
5. Once it becomes brown, add coriander and chili powder.
6. Add salt to taste.
7. Add ginger paste, mixture of fried onions and yogurt, let it cook for a minute.
8. Then put garam masala and saffron for flavor.
9. The masala should fuse well with the chicken.
10. Cover it and give it some time to cook on low heat.
11. Let it cook for ten minutes.
12. Garnish it with coriander.
13. Your dish is ready to be served.

- **Wok Indian Butter Chicken**

Preparation Time: 15 minutes

Cooking Time: 30 minutes

Serving: 5

Ingredients:

- Butter, one cup
- Ginger paste, one tsp.
- Chicken, one pound
- Garam masala, half tsp.
- Coriander powder, one tsp.

- Chili powder, one tbsp.
- Cardamom, six
- Garlic paste, one tsp.
- Yoghurt, one cup
- Salt, to taste
- Coriander, as required
- Onion, two
- Saffron, a pinch

Instructions:

1. Heat the butter into a pan.
2. Put cardamom, cloves, garlic and fry the mix properly.
3. Then add the chicken and let it cook for about two minutes.
4. Once it becomes brown, add coriander and chili powder.
5. Add salt to taste.
6. Add ginger paste, mixture of fried onions and yogurt, let it cook for a minute.
7. Then put garam masala and saffron for flavor.
8. The masala should fuse well with the chicken.
9. Cover it and give it some time to cook on slow flame.
10. Let it cook for ten minutes.
11. Garnish it with coriander.
12. Your dish is ready to be served.

- **Wok Indian Roasted Vegetables**

Preparation Time: 10 minutes

Cooking Time: 20 minutes

Serving: 4

Ingredients:

- Mixed vegetables, two cups
- Garlic, two
- Garlic, one slice
- Mixed Indian spice, two tbsp.
- Tomato puree, half cup
- Liquid ghee, half cup

Instructions:

1. Cut the vegetables.
2. Mince the garlic and ginger.
3. Add the tomato puree, spices, minced garlic and ginger to a medium bowl.
4. Stir in the liquid ghee or oil and cook the mixture in a wok.
5. Add the vegetables and mix to coat.
6. Spread the vegetables into one layer on the prepared sheet pan and season with salt and pepper.
7. Roast in the oven for twenty minutes or until the veggies are cooked.
8. Your dish is ready to be served.

- **Wok Indian Egg Fried Rice**

Preparation Time: 10 minutes

Cooking Time: 30 minutes

Serving Size: 4

Ingredients:

- Egg, one
- Soy sauce, half cup
- Cooked rice, three cups
- Tomatoes, two
- Cilantro, half cup
- Salt and pepper, to taste
- Vegetable oil, two tbsp.
- Indian chili peppers, three
- Toasted walnuts, half cup
- Onion, one
- Scallions, half cup
- Minced garlic, one tsp.

Instructions:

1. Heat a large nonstick wok over high heat.
2. When the wok is very hot, add two tsp. of the oil.
3. Add the eggs, pinch of salt and cook for a minute or two until done.
4. Add the remaining oil to the wok and add the onion, scallions and garlic.
5. Sauté for a minute, add the chili pepper if using, tomatoes and stir in all the rice.
6. Add the soy sauce and stir to mix all the ingredients.
7. Keep stirring a few minutes, and then add egg back to the wok.
8. Adjust soy sauce if needed and stir well another thirty seconds.

9. Your dish is ready to be served.

- **Wok Kadai Chole**

Preparation Time: 5 minutes

Cooking Time: 25 minutes

Serving: 4

Ingredients:

- Ginger, one slice
- Cinnamon stick, one
- Cumin, one tsp.
- Garlic, two
- Green chili, two
- Coriander powder, one tsp.
- Paprika powder, one tsp.
- Vegetable oil, one tbsp.
- Sliced onion, one
- Chickpeas, boiled, two cups
- Potatoes, two
- Lemon juice, two tbsp.
- Chopped tomatoes, one cup

Instructions:

1. Blend together the ginger, garlic, half green chili, coriander, cumin and paprika.
2. Heat oil in a wok over medium high heat.
3. Add cinnamon stick and bay leaf and cook for a few seconds.

4. Add the blended mixture to the wok.

5. Blend the tomatoes into a puree and add to the wok.

6. Add the chickpeas, potatoes, a cup of water and half teaspoon of salt.

7. Cover, reduce heat to medium and cook for ten minutes.

8. Add in the peppers, ginger, paprika, lemon juice, half a green chili chopped and garam masala.

9. Taste and adjust the salt and heat.

10. Garnish with sliced onion, chopped tomato, smoked paprika and a dash of lemon juice and cilantro.

11. Your dish is ready to be served.

Chapter 3: Wok Dinner Recipes

Following are some amazing dinner Thai, Chinese, and Indian recipes that you can follow by using a wok:

3.1 Wok Chinese Dinner Recipes

- **Wok Chinese Chicken and Broccoli**

Preparation Time: 10 minutes

Cooking Time: 5 minutes

Serving: 4

Ingredients:

- Soy sauce, two tbsp.
- Broccoli, two cups
- Chicken, two pounds
- Vegetable oil, two tbsp.

- Cornstarch, two tbsp.
- Sesame oil, two tbsp.
- Sugar, one tsp.
- Oyster sauce, two tbsp.
- Pepper to taste
- Salt, as required
- Chinese cooking wine, two tsp.

Instructions:

1. Add the oil in a wok.
2. Add in the chicken and cook it properly.
3. Remove the chicken from the wok.
4. Next add the Broccoli and cook it.
5. Add the chicken and rest of the ingredients.
6. In the end add the cornstarch and once the dish thickens switch off the heat.
7. Your dish is ready to be served.

- **Wok Chinese Crispy Sesame Chicken**

Preparation Time: 15 minutes

Cooking Time: 15 minutes

Serving: 6

Ingredients:

- Boneless chicken thighs, two pounds
- Sesame oil, two tbsp.
- Corn starch, half cup
- Water, half cup

- Egg, one
- Soy sauce, a quarter cup
- Brown sugar, two tbsp.
- Sesame seeds, one tsp.
- Crushed red pepper, one tsp.
- Minced garlic, one tsp.
- Vegetable oil, for frying

Instructions:

1. Mix all the liquid ingredients.
2. Add the chicken pieces to the batter and coat.
3. Fry the chicken pieces.
4. To make the sauce, mix all the ingredients together.
5. In a large wok add the sesame oil to the frying pan and add the garlic and red pepper flakes and cook for thirty seconds.
6. Add in the sauce and the chicken and coat quickly.
7. Your dish is ready to be served.

- **Wok Chinese Stir Fried Sichuan Chicken**

Preparation Time: 20 minutes

Cooking Time: 15 minutes

Serving: 4

Ingredients:

- All-purpose flour, half cup
- Egg, one
- Oil, one tbsp.
- Sichuan pepper, two

- Chicken, two pounds
- Ginger, one slice
- Soy sauce, two tbsp.
- Wine, one tsp.
- Dried chilies, two
- Garlic, two
- Chicken cubes, two
- Vegetable oil, for frying

Instructions:

1. Heat up some oil for deep frying.
2. Dip the chicken into the batter and deep fry until golden brown.
3. Transfer out to a plate lined with paper towels.
4. In a wok, heat up some oil until smoky hot.
5. Add in the sliced ginger, garlic, and stir fry until they turn light brown.
6. Add in the dried chilies, Sichuan pepper and quickly stir until you smell the spicy and fragrant aroma.
7. Add in the chicken cubes, soy sauce, and wine.
8. Add salt to taste.
9. Your dish is ready to be served.

- **Wok Chinese Peanuts and Chicken**

Preparation Time: 10 minutes

Cooking Time: 5 minutes

Serving: 4

Ingredients:

- Soy sauce, two tbsp.
- Peanuts, one cup
- Chicken, two pounds
- Vegetable oil, two tbsp.
- Cornstarch, two tbsp.
- Sesame oil, two tbsp.
- Sugar, one tsp.
- Oyster sauce, two tbsp.
- Pepper to taste
- Salt, as required
- Chinese cooking wine, two tsp.

Instructions:

1. Add oil in a wok.
2. Add in the beef and cook it properly.
3. Remove the chicken from the wok.
4. Next add the peanuts and cook it.
5. Add the chicken and rest of the ingredients.
6. In the end add the cornstarch and once the dish thickens, switch off the heat.
7. Your dish is ready to be served.

- **Wok Chinese Vegetable and Chicken Stir Fry**

Preparation Time: 5 minutes

Cooking Time: 25 minutes

Serving Size: 3

Ingredients:

- Coleslaw mix, one bag
- Green onions, a quarter cup
- Shredded carrots, half cup
- Honey roasted peanuts, half cup
- Oil, three tbsp.
- Cooked chicken, one pound
- Linguini noodles, five ounces
- Cilantro, a quarter cup
- Soy sauce, one tbsp.
- Honey, five tbsp.
- Sesame oil, three tbsp.
- Red chili flakes, two tbsp.
- Minced garlic, four

Instructions:

1. Cook linguini noodles according to package instructions.
2. While noodles are being cooked whisk together in a small bowl the soy sauce, honey, sesame oil, garlic and red pepper flakes.
3. Pour sauce onto drained noodles, and toss together.
4. Add the cooked chicken, shredded cabbage, shredded carrots and shredded cilantro to noodle mixture and mix.
5. Then gently stir in half of the chopped cilantro, green onions and peanuts, reserving the other half for garnish.
6. Your dish is ready to be served.

3.2 Wok Thai Dinner Recipes

- **Wok Thai Gai Pad King**

Preparation Time: 5 minutes

Cooking Time: 5 minutes

Serving: 2

Ingredients:

- Dried mushrooms, half cup
- Chicken, one pound
- Garlic, two
- Soy sauce, two tbsp.
- Thai chilies, two
- Ginger, one slice
- Oyster sauce, two tsp.
- Chicken stock, two tbsp.

Instructions:

1. Soak dried mushroom in hot water for at least fifteen minutes.
2. Mix the chicken with two teaspoons of soy sauce.
3. Combine all the sauce ingredients.
4. In a wok, sauté chopped garlic and Thai chilies in a little cooking oil.
5. Turn the heat up to high, add the chicken and mix it with the herbs.
6. Add the sauce, the ginger, mushrooms, onion, and red bell pepper.

7. Mix everything together until the chicken is fully cooked through.

8. Add the green onions.

9. Your dish is ready to be served.

- **Wok Thai Cashew Chicken**

Preparation Time: 15 minutes

Cooking Time: 15 minutes

Serving: 2

Ingredients:

- Chicken, one pound
- Water, half cup
- Garlic, two
- Oyster sauce, two tbsp.
- Soy sauce, two tbsp.
- Red pepper flakes, half tsp.
- Raw cashews, half cup
- Corn starch, one tbsp.
- Sesame oil, one tsp.
- Vegetable oil, two tbsp.
- Green onions, half cup
- Onion, one
- Tomatoes, half cup

Instructions:

1. In a wok add the vegetable oil and cook the chicken.

2. Once cooked, remove the chicken from the wok and add in the onions.

3. Add the tomatoes and rest of the spices.

4. Add the chicken back to the wok.

5. Add the sesame oil and cashews and cook for ten minutes.

6. Add the green onions and corn starch.

7. Cook for five minutes and dish out.

8. Your dish is ready to be served.

- **Wok Thai Basil Chicken**

Preparation Time: 5 minutes

Cooking Time: 20 minutes

Serving Size: 6

Ingredients:

- Fresh Thai basil leaves, two cups
- Oyster sauce, two tsp.
- Honey, two tbsp.
- Boneless chicken, two pounds
- Brown sugar, two tbsp.
- Salt and pepper to taste
- Canola oil, one tsp.
- Lime juice, two tbsp.
- Lime wedges, 4
- Crushed red chili flakes, two tsp.
- Fish sauce, two tsp.
- Minced garlic, two tbsp.

Instructions:

1. In a large bowl, stir together sliced chicken, oyster sauce, soy sauce, fish sauce, lime juice and brown sugar until evenly coated.

2. Allow chicken to marinate while preparing the rest of the meal.

3. Heat canola oil in a large wok over medium-high heat.

4. Add garlic and red pepper flakes and sauté until fragrant for about thirty seconds.

5. Add chicken and sauce and increase the heat to high.

6. Cook, stirring frequently, until chicken is cooked through and no longer pink for about five minutes.

7. Add basil leaves and continue to cook, stirring occasionally, until basil leaves get wilted for about four minutes.

8. Your dish is ready to be served.

- **Wok Thai Ginger Chicken**

Preparation Time: 15 minutes

Cooking Time: 15 minutes

Serving: 2

Ingredients:

- Chicken, one pound
- Water, half cup
- Garlic, two
- Oyster sauce, two tbsp.
- Soy sauce, two tbsp.
- Red pepper flakes, half tsp.

- Ginger Julian, a quarter cup
- Corn starch, one tbsp.
- Sesame oil, one tsp.
- Vegetable oil, two tbsp.
- Green onions, half cup
- Onion, one
- Tomatoes, half cup

Instructions:

1. In a wok, add the vegetable oil and cook the chicken.
2. Once cooked, remove the chicken from the wok and add in the onions.
3. Add the tomatoes and rest of the spices.
4. Add the chicken back to the wok.
5. Add the ginger as well as sesame oil and cook for ten minutes.
6. Add the green onions and corn starch.
7. Cook for five minutes and dish out.
8. Your dish is ready to be served.

- **Wok Thai Chicken Stir Fry with Basil and Mint**

Preparation Time: 15 minutes

Cooking Time: 15 minutes

Serving: 2

Ingredients:

- Chicken, one pound
- Water, half cup
- Garlic, two

- Oyster sauce, two tbsp.
- Soy sauce, two tbsp.
- Red pepper flakes, half tsp.
- Basil leaves, half cup
- Mint leaves, half cup
- Corn starch, one tbsp.
- Sesame oil, one tsp.
- Vegetable oil, two tbsp.
- Green onions, half cup
- Onion, one
- Tomatoes, half cup

Instructions:

1. In a wok add the vegetable oil and cook the chicken.
2. Once cooked, remove the chicken from the wok and add in the onions.
3. Add the tomatoes and rest of the spices.
4. Add the chicken back to the wok.
5. Add the sesame oil and cook for ten minutes.
6. Add the green onions and corn starch.
7. In the end, add the basil and mint leaves.
8. Cook for five minutes and dish out.
9. Your dish is ready to be served.

3.3 Wok Indian Dinner Recipes

- **Wok Indian Sweet and Sour Chicken Curry**

Preparation Time: 5 minutes

Cooking Time: 20 minutes

Serving: 4

Ingredients:

- Chicken, two pounds
- Tomato puree, half cup
- Salt, as required
- Garlic, two
- Garam masala (allspice), half tsp.
- Yoghurt, one cup
- Sugar, two tbsp.
- Mango chutney, two tbsp.
- Chili powder, one tsp.
- Vegetable oil, half cup
- Chilies, two
- Cream, half cup

Instructions:

1. In a large bowl mix together the tomato puree with the yogurt, garam masala, chili powder, garlic, mango chutney, salt and sugar.

2. Heat the oil in a wok, pour in the spice mix, stir, reduce the heat and cook for two minutes.

3. Add the chicken, stir to coat all of the pieces and add the water.

4. Add half of the chilies and cream.

5. Serve garnished with chopped coriander leaves.

6. Your dish is ready to be served.

- **Wok Indian Spiced Chicken and Capsicum Stir Fry**

Preparation Time: 5 minutes

Cooking Time: 15 minutes

Serving: 4

Ingredients:

- Chicken, two pounds
- Tomato puree, half cup
- Salt, as required
- Garlic, two
- Capsicum, two cups
- Mix spice, four tbsp.
- Vegetable oil, half cup
- Chilies, two
- Onion, one cup

Instructions:

1. Heat the oil in a wok, add the onions and cook for two minutes.

2. Add the garlic and tomato puree.

3. Add the spice mix, stir, reduce the heat and cook for two minutes.

4. Add the chicken, stir to coat all of the pieces and add the water.

5. Add half of the chilies and capsicum.

6. Serve garnished with chopped coriander leaves.

7. Your dish is ready to be served.

- **Wok Indian Cauliflower Fried Rice with Chicken**

Preparation Time: 10 minutes

Cooking Time: 5 minutes

Serving: 4

Ingredients:

- Soy sauce, two tbsp.
- Mixed spice, two tbsp.
- Chicken, two pounds
- Vegetable oil, two tbsp.
- Cornstarch, two tbsp.
- Sesame oil, two tbsp.
- Cauliflower, one cup
- Sugar, one tsp.
- Oyster sauce, two tbsp.
- Pepper to taste
- Salt, as required
- Chinese cooking wine, two tsp.

Instructions:

1. Add the oil in a wok.

2. Add in the chicken and cook it properly.

3. Add the chicken, cauliflower and rest of the ingredients.

4. In the end add the cornstarch and once the dish thickens switch off the heat.

5. Your dish is ready to be served.

- **Wok Indian Chicken Tikka Masala**

Preparation Time: 5 minutes

Cooking Time: 15 minutes

Serving: 4

Ingredients:

- Chicken, two pounds
- Tomato puree, half cup
- Salt, as required
- Garlic, two
- Tikka masala, four tbsp.
- Vegetable oil, half cup
- Chilies, two
- Onion, one cup

Instructions:

1. Heat the oil in a wok, add the onions and cook for two minutes.
2. Add the garlic and tomato puree.
3. Add the tikka masala, stir, reduce the heat and cook for two minutes.
4. Add the chicken, stir to coat all of the pieces and add the water.
5. Serve garnished with chopped chilies and coriander leaves.
6. Your dish is ready to be served.

- **Wok Indian Seared Chicken**

Preparation Time: 5 minutes

Cooking Time: 25 minutes

Serving: 4

Ingredients:

- Ginger, one slice
- Cinnamon stick, one
- Cumin, one tsp.
- Garlic, two
- Green chili, two
- Coriander powder, one tsp.
- Paprika powder, one tsp.
- Vegetable oil, one tbsp.
- Chicken, two pounds
- Lemon juice, two tbsp.
- Chopped tomatoes, one cup

Instructions:

1. Blend together the ginger, garlic, half green chili, coriander, cumin and paprika.
2. Heat oil in a wok over medium high heat.
3. Add cinnamon stick and bay leaf and cook for a few seconds.
4. Add the blended mixture to the wok.
5. Blend the tomatoes into the puree and add to the wok.
6. Add the chicken into the mixture and cook.

7. Add in the peppers, ginger, paprika, lemon juice, half a green chili chopped and garam masala.

8. Taste and adjust the salt and heat.

9. Garnish with cilantro.

10. Your dish is ready to be served.

Chapter 4: Wok Snack Recipes

Following are some very easy snack Thai, Chinese, and Indian recipes that you can follow by using a wok:

4.1 Wok Chinese Snack Recipes

- **Wok Chinese Fried Peanuts**

Preparation Time: 35 minutes

Cooking Time: 10 minutes

Serving: 6

Ingredients:

- Sea salt, as required

- Flavored oil, as required

- Peanuts, six ounces

Instructions:

1. Place the peanuts in a strainer or colander, and rinse under water.
2. In a clean wok, add in the air-dried peanuts and enough oil to just cover the peanuts.
3. Then turn on the heat to medium low.
4. Cook for ten minutes.
5. Strain the peanuts out, and spread them out on a baking sheet to cool completely. Sprinkle with salt.
6. Your dish is ready to be served.

- **Wok Chinese Glazed Greens with Oyster Sauce**

Preparation Time: 5 minutes

Cooking Time: 5 minutes

Serving: 2

Ingredients:

- Oyster sauce, one tbsp.
- Chinese greens, two cups
- Vegetable oil, half tbsp.

Instructions:

1. Fill a wok with water and bring to a rapid boil.
2. Add the vegetables to the pan and allow boiling for five minutes until tender.
3. Drain and place on a large serving plate.
4. Cut the vegetables into bite-sized pieces.
5. Heat the vegetable oil in a wok until smoking-hot and pour over the top of the greens.
6. Your dish is ready to be served with oyster sauce.

- **Wok Fried Soy Cheung Fun**

Preparation Time: 15 minutes

Cooking Time: 15 minutes

Serving: 2

Ingredients:

- Minced garlic, one
- Cheung fun noodles, one pack
- Minced pork, one cup
- Rapeseed oil, one tsp.
- Shaoxing wine, one tsp.
- Sesame seeds, one tbsp.
- Soy sauce, one tbsp.

Instructions:

1. Heat the wok on medium heat.
2. Add the rapeseed oil and minced garlic, stir fry until lightly golden.
3. Add the minced pork to the wok.
4. Add in the cheung fun noodles, with the rest of the ingredients.
5. Turn up the heat and toss all ingredients repeatedly for five minutes.
6. Garnish with freshly ground sesame seeds.
7. Your dish is ready to be served.

- **Wok Chinese Dumplings**

Preparation Time: 15 minutes

Cooking Time: 20 minutes

Serving: 2

Ingredients:

- Dumpling dough, one cup
- Pork mince, one cup
- Garlic and ginger paste, one tbsp.
- Chinese mushrooms, half cup
- Coriander, as required.
- Soy sauce, one tsp.
- Vegetable oil, two tbsp.

Instructions:

1. Mix all the filling ingredients.
2. Add the mixture in the dumpling dough.
3. In a wok add the oil and place the dumpling.
4. Cook it until golden brown.
5. Your dish is ready to be served.

- **Wok Kok Chai**

Preparation Time: 15 minutes

Cooking Time: 15 minutes

Serving: 2

Ingredients:

- Dumpling dough, one cup
- Peanuts, one cup
- Sesame oil, one tsp.
- Sugar, a quarter cup
- Vegetable oil, two tbsp.

Instructions:

1. Mix all the filling ingredients.
2. Add the mixture in the dumpling dough.
3. In a wok add the oil and place the dumpling.
4. Cook it until golden brown.
5. Your dish is ready to be served.

4.2 Wok Thai Snack Recipes

- **Wok Thai Sausage Bite**

Preparation Time: 5 minutes

Cooking Time: 5 minutes

Serving: 2

Ingredients:

- Sausage, one cup
- Oyster sauce, as required
- Vegetable oil, for frying

Instructions:

1. Cut the sausage into bite sizes.
2. Fry the sausage.
3. Serve it with oyster sauce.

- **Wok Thai Pork and Sweet Corn Snack**

Preparation Time: 5 minutes

Cooking Time: 5 minutes

Serving: 2

Ingredients:

- Pork mince, one cup
- Vegetable oil, one tbsp.
- Corn, one cup
- Soy sauce, one tbsp.
- Oyster sauce, one tbsp.

Instructions:

1. In a large wok add all the things together.
2. Let it cook for five minutes.
3. Your dish is ready to be served.

- **Wok Thai Spring Rolls**

Preparation Time: 15 minutes

Cooking Time: 10 minutes

Serving: 2

Ingredients:

- Dumpling dough, one cup
- Pork mince, one cup
- Garlic and ginger paste, one tbsp.
- Coriander, as required.
- Soy sauce, one tsp.
- Vegetable oil, two tbsp.

Instructions:

1. Mix all the filling ingredients.
2. Add the mixture in the spring roll sheets.
3. In a wok add the oil and place the rolls.
4. Cook it until golden brown.

5. Your dish is ready to be served.

- **Wok Thai Red Curry Lime Wings**

Preparation Time: 60 minutes

Cooking Time: 20 minutes

Serving: 6-8

Ingredients:

- Red curry paste, half cup
- Garlic powder, half tsp.
- Pepper powder, half tsp.
- Flour, two cups
- Butter, half cup
- Vegetable oil, for frying
- Chicken breasts, cut into small pieces
- Cayenne pepper, one tsp.
- Paprika powder, one tsp.
- Salt, one tsp.

Instructions:

1. Trim the wings and cut into one-inch chunks.
2. Combine the flour, paprika, cayenne pepper, and salt in a big bowl.
3. Mix together in a separate bowl, one cup butter, half cup red curry paste, a dash of garlic powder and a dash of pepper.
4. Put the chicken wings into the large bowl of flour mixture, coating each wing evenly.

5. Dip into mixture of butter and hot sauce, then again into flour mixture.

6. Add oil in a deep fryer and heat it to 375 degrees.

7. Fry them for ten to fifteen minutes or until some parts of the wings begin to turn dark brown.

8. Your chicken wings are ready to be served.

- **Wok Thai Deep Fried Prawn Cake**

Preparation Time: 15 minutes

Cooking Time: 10 minutes

Serving: 2

Ingredients:

- Prawn, half pound
- All-purpose flour, one cup
- Corn flour, half cup
- Mix Thai spice, one tsp.
- Vegetable oil, for frying
- Egg, one

Instructions:

1. Mix all the dried ingredients together.

2. Add the prawns into the egg mixture first and then coat it in the dried ingredients.

3. Fry each prawn.

4. Your dish is ready to be served with your preferred sauce.

4.3 Wok Indian Snack Recipes

- **Wok Indian Tadka Bread**

Preparation Time: 10 minutes

Cooking Time: 20 minutes

Serving: 2

Ingredients:

- Lemon juice, two tbsp.
- Bread, four slices.
- Vegetable oil, one tsp.
- Turmeric, half tsp.
- Cumin powder, half tsp.
- Sugar, one tbsp.
- Onion, half cup
- Mustard seeds, one tsp.
- Yoghurt, half cup
- Chilies, four

Instructions:

1. Heat the oil in a wok, and then add the mustard seeds.
2. Once they are popped, tip in the onion and chilies.
3. Then add the turmeric, sugar, cumin and salt and continue to fry.
4. Pour in the yogurt and lemon juice, stirring continuously.
5. Lastly, fold in the bread carefully.
6. Your dish is ready to be served.

• Wok Batata Wada

Preparation Time: 20 minutes

Cooking Time: 25 minutes

Serving: 12

Ingredients:

- Milk, half cup
- Flour, half cup
- Cooking oil, as required
- Potatoes, four large
- Onion, one
- Coriander, as required
- Indiana mix spice, one tsp.

Instructions:

1. Mix the boiled potatoes, onion, coriander, and Indian spice mix.
2. Make small round balls out of it.
3. Make the batter.
4. Dip the balls in the batter and fry it.
5. Your dish is ready to be served.

• Wok Coconut Milk Sambhar

Preparation Time: 10 minutes

Cooking Time: 20 minutes

Serving: 4

Ingredients:

- Coconut milk, one cup

- Mixed vegetables, two cups
- Curry leaves, as required
- Coriander leaves, as required
- Mustard seeds, one tsp.
- Chilies, one tsp.
- Black pepper, as required
- Salt, as required

Instructions:

1. Heat oil in a wok and temper mustard seeds, red chilies and black pepper.
2. Add the rest of the vegetables.
3. Pour coconut milk and boil for two minutes.
4. Garnish with curry leaves and coriander leaves.
5. Your dish is ready to be served.

- **Wok Indian Deep Fried Puffy Bread**

Preparation Time: 10 minutes

Cooking Time: 5 minutes

Serving: 2

Ingredients:

- Semolina flour, two tbsp.
- All-purpose flour, one cup
- Salt, as required
- Oil, for frying

Instructions:

1. Mix all the ingredients together and make small tortilla size breads into it.

2. Fry the bread.

3. You can serve it with any gravy you like.

- **Wok Badam Barfi**

Preparation Time: 5 minutes

Cooking Time: 12 minutes

Serving: 2

Ingredients:

- Almond flour, one cup

- Sugar, one cup

- Rose water, two tbsp.

- Cardamom powder, half tsp.

- Water, one cup

- Ghee, half cup

Instructions:

1. Sift the almond flour.

2. Add sugar, water, rose water and cardamom powder in a pan and cook on medium heat.

3. Stir and let the sugar dissolve and mixture come to a boil.

4. As soon as the mixture starts boiling, add the almond flour.

5. Add a teaspoon of ghee and mix.

6. Keep stirring the mixture using a spatula on low heat.

7. After around five minutes, it will start leaving the sides of the pan.

8. Your dish is ready to be served.

Chapter 5: Wok Vegetarian Recipes

Following are some very easy vegetarian Thai, Chinese, and Indian recipes that you can follow by using a wok:

5.1 Wok Chinese Vegetarian Recipes

- **Wok Chinese Creamy Peanut Sauce Stir Fry**

Preparation Time: 20 minutes

Cooking Time: 15 minutes

Serving: 4

Ingredients:

- All-purpose flour, half cup
- Egg, one
- Oil, one tbsp.
- Sichuan pepper, two
- Mixed vegetables, two cups

- Ginger, one slice
- Soy sauce, two tbsp.
- Wine, one tsp.
- Dried chilies, two
- Garlic, two
- Creamy peanut sauce, two tbsp.
- Vegetable oil, for frying

Instructions:

1. In a wok, heat up some oil until smoky hot.
2. Add in the sliced ginger, garlic, and stir fry until they turn light brown.
3. Add in the mixed vegetables, dried chilies, Sichuan peppercorns and quickly stir until you smell the spicy and fragrant aroma.
4. Add in the creamy peanut sauce, soy sauce, and wine.
5. Add salt to taste.
6. Your dish is ready to be served.

- **Wok Chinese Ginger Veggie Stir Fry**

Preparation Time: 15 minutes

Cooking Time: 15 minutes

Serving: 2

Ingredients:

- Mixed vegetables, one cup
- Water, half cup
- Garlic, two
- Oyster sauce, two tbsp.

- Soy sauce, two tbsp.
- Red pepper flakes, half tsp.
- Ginger Julian, a quarter cup
- Corn starch, one tbsp.
- Sesame oil, one tsp.
- Vegetable oil, two tbsp.
- Green onions, half cup
- Onion, one
- Tomatoes, half cup

Instructions:

1. In a wok add the vegetable oil and cook the vegetables.
2. Once cooked, remove the vegetables from the wok and add in the onions.
3. Add the tomatoes and rest of the spices.
4. Add the vegetables back to the wok.
5. Add the ginger as well as sesame oil and cook for ten minutes.
6. Add the green onions and corn starch.
7. Cook for five minutes and dish out.
8. Your dish is ready to be served.

- **Wok Chinese Stir Fry in Black Bean Sauce**

Preparation Time: 20 minutes

Cooking Time: 15 minutes

Serving: 4

Ingredients:

- All-purpose flour, half cup

- Egg, one
- Oil, one tbsp.
- Sichuan pepper, two
- Mixed vegetables, two cups
- Ginger, one slice
- Soy sauce, two tbsp.
- Wine, one tsp.
- Dried chilies, two
- Garlic, two
- Black bean sauce, two tbsp.
- Vegetable oil, for frying

Instructions:

1. In a wok, heat up some oil until smoky hot.
2. Add in the sliced ginger, garlic, and stir fry until they turn light brown.
3. Add in the mixed vegetables, dried chilies, Sichuan peppercorns and quickly stir until you smell the spicy and fragrant aroma.
4. Add in the black bean sauce, soy sauce, and wine.
5. Add salt to taste.
6. Your dish is ready to be served.

- **Wok Chinese Tofu Stir Fry with Garlic Sauce**

Preparation Time: 10 minutes

Cooking Time: 40 minutes

Serving Size: 4

Ingredients:

- Brown sugar, one tbsp.
- Soy sauce, a quarter cup
- Fish sauce, one tbsp.
- Chili garlic sauce, one tbsp.
- Oil, two tbsp.
- Mixed vegetables, two cups
- Rice noodles, half pound
- Minced garlic, one tsp.

Instructions:

1. Pour noodles into bowl and cover with hot tap water.
2. Soak for twenty minutes.
3. Heat oil in a large wok over medium-high heat.
4. Add garlic and stir fry until golden.
5. Add fish sauce or salt and vegetables.
6. Stir fry until done.
7. Add soy sauce, chili pepper sauce, and brown sugar.
8. Mix until sugar is dissolved.
9. Stir fry noodles until firm but tender.
10. Your dish is ready to be served.

- **Wok Chinese Vegetable Stir Fry**

Preparation Time: 10 minutes

Cooking Time: 5 minutes

Serving: 4

Ingredients:

- Soy sauce, two tbsp.
- Mixed vegetables, two cups
- Vegetable oil, two tbsp.
- Cornstarch, two tbsp.
- Sesame oil, two tbsp.
- Sugar, one tsp.
- Oyster sauce, two tbsp.
- Pepper to taste
- Salt, as required
- Chinese cooking wine, two tsp.

Instructions:

1. Add the oil in a wok.
2. Add in the vegetables and cook it properly.
3. In the end add the cornstarch and one the dish thickens switch off the heat.
4. Your dish is ready to be served.

5.2 Wok Thai Vegetarian Recipes

- **Wok Spicy Thai Coconut Stir Fry**

Preparation Time: 15 minutes

Cooking Time: 10 minutes

Serving: 4

Ingredients:

- Mixed vegetables, two cups
- Peanut butter, two tbsp.

- Coconut milk, one cup
- Soy sauce, two tbsp.
- Brown sugar, one tbsp.
- Minced garlic, one tsp.
- Ginger, one slice
- Sirarcha sauce, one tsp.
- Vegetable oil, three tbsp.

Instructions:

1. Heat the cooking oil in a large wok over medium high heat.

2. Once hot, add the vegetables to the skillet in order of hardest to softest to allow harder vegetables, like carrots, more Time to cook and to avoid over cooking softer vegetables.

3. Stir fry the vegetables.

4. In a medium bowl, whisk together the coconut milk, peanut butter, sriracha, brown sugar, soy sauce, lime juice, minced garlic, and grated ginger.

5. Pour the prepared spicy coconut sauce over the vegetables.

6. Cook for ten minutes.

7. Your dish is ready to be served.

- **Wok Thai Drunken Noodles**

Preparation Time: 5 minutes

Cooking Time: 15 minutes

Serving Size: 2

Ingredients:

- Green onion, one
- Bell pepper, one
- Thai basil, a handful
- Garlic and ginger paste, one tsp.
- Sesame oil, two tbsp.
- Soy sauce, one tsp.
- Oyster sauce, one tsp.
- Fish sauce, one tsp.
- Salt and black pepper, to taste
- Red Thai chili, one
- Shallots, half cup

Instructions:

1. Cook the vegetables in the sesame oil.
2. Add spices and sauces into the mixture and then add the noodles and mix thoroughly.
3. Your dish is ready to be served.

- **Wok Vegan Thai Red Curry**

Preparation Time: 15 minutes

Cooking Time: 40 minutes

Serving Size: 4

Ingredients:

- Salt, a pinch
- Red bell pepper, one
- Coconut milk, one cup

- Red bell pepper, one
- Thai red curry paste, four tbsp.
- Butternut squash, one
- Vegetable oil, two tbsp.
- Chili, one tsp.
- Water, half cup
- Shallots, half cup
- Brown rice, four

Instructions:

1. Add the shallots with a pinch of salt and fry for ten minutes over a medium heat until softened and beginning to caramelize.
2. Add the red curry paste and chili to the dish and fry for two mins.
3. Tip in the squash and pepper, and then stir through the coconut milk along with half cup water.
4. Season and stir through half of the coriander.
5. Spoon the curry into deep bowls, scatter with the remaining coriander and serve with rice and lime wedges for squeezing over.

- **Wok Vegan Pad Thai**

Preparation Time: 5 minutes

Cooking Time: 15 minutes

Serving Size: 4

Ingredients:

- Chopped green onions, three
- Fresh bean sprouts, half cup

- Garlic cloves, three
- Oil, three tbsp.
- Limes, two
- Red bell pepper, one
- Flat rice noodles, eight ounces
- Dry roasted peanuts, two cups
- Soy sauce, one tbsp.
- Light brown sugar, five tbsp.
- Fish sauce, three tbsp.
- Creamy peanut butter, two tbsp.
- Rice vinegar, two tbsp.
- Sirarcha hot sauce, one tbsp.

Instructions:

1. Cook noodles according to package instructions, just until tender.
2. Rinse under cold water.
3. Mix the sauce ingredients together.
4. Add garlic and bell pepper in a wok.
5. Push everything to the side of the pan.
6. Add noodles, sauce, bean sprouts and peanuts to the pan.
7. Toss everything to combine.
8. Top with green onions, extra peanuts, cilantro and lime wedges.
9. Your dish is ready to be served.

• Wok Vegetables in Hot Garlic Sauce

Preparation Time: 15 minutes

Cooking Time: 20 minutes

Serving: 4

Ingredients:

- Ginger, one slice
- Sesame oil, two tbsp.
- Red chilies, two
- Garlic, two
- Onion, one
- White vinegar, two tbsp.
- Hot garlic sauce, two tbsp.
- Mixed vegetables, two cups
- Salt, to taste
- Pepper, to taste
- Corn flour, two tbsp.
- Spring onion, half cup
- Crushed peanuts, a quarter cup

Instructions:

1. Heat sesame oil in a wok.
2. Add finely chopped garlic, whole red chilies, ginger and celery.
3. Give it a quick stir for a minute to release the aroma of the herbs.
4. Add diced onion and stir-fry for a minute or till onion become translucent.

5. Pour white vinegar and mix nicely the ingredients to glaze the pan.

6. Next, add the hot garlic sauce mix.

7. Add salt and pepper.

8. Now, add the corn flour slurry or paste and continuously stir the sauce to avoid any lump formation.

9. Garnish the gravy with spring onion, crushed peanuts and

10. Your dish is ready to be served.

- **Wok Stir Fried Noodles**

Preparation Time: 5 minutes

Cooking Time: 25 minutes

Serving Size: 3

Ingredients:

- Coleslaw mix, one bag
- Green onions, a quarter cup
- Shredded carrots, half cup
- Honey roasted peanuts, half cup
- Oil, three tbsp.
- Linguini noodles, five ounces
- Cilantro, a quarter cup
- Soy sauce, one tbsp.
- Honey, five tbsp.
- Sesame oil, three tbsp.
- Red chili flakes, two tbsp.

- Minced garlic, four

Instructions:

1. Cook the noodles.

2. While noodles are being cooked, whisk together in a small bowl the soy sauce, honey, sesame oil, garlic and red pepper flakes.

3. Pour sauce onto drained noodles, and toss together.

4. Add shredded cabbage, shredded carrots and shredded cilantro to the noodle mixture and mix.

5. Then gently stir in half of chopped cilantro, green onions and peanuts, reserving the other half for garnish.

6. Your dish is ready to be served.

- **Wok Tofu Stir Fry**

Preparation Time: 10 minutes

Cooking Time: 40 minutes

Serving Size: 4

Ingredients:

- Brown sugar, one tbsp.

- Soy sauce, a quarter cup

- Oyster sauce, one tbsp.

- Chili garlic sauce, one tbsp.

- Oil, two tbsp.

- Tofu, two cups

- Rice noodles, half pound

- Minced garlic, one tsp.

Instructions:

1. Pour noodles into bowl and cover with hot tap water.

2. Heat oil in a large wok over medium-high heat.

3. Add garlic, tofu and stir fry until golden.

4. Add oyster sauce or salt and vegetables.

5. Stir fry until done.

6. Add soy sauce, chili pepper sauce, and brown sugar.

7. Mix until sugar is dissolved.

8. Stir fry noodles until firm but tender.

9. Your dish is ready to be served.

5.3 Wok Indian Vegetarian Recipes

- **Wok Indian Quinoa and Chickpea Stir Fry**

Preparation Time: 10 minutes

Cooking Time: 15 minutes

Serving: 4

Ingredients:

- Quinoa, two cups
- Tomato puree, half cup
- Salt, as required
- Garlic, two
- Chickpea, two cups
- Mix spice, four tbsp.
- Vegetable oil, half cup

- Chilies, two
- Onion, one cup

Instructions:

1. Heat the oil in a wok, add the onions and cook for two minutes.
2. Add the garlic and tomato puree.
3. Add the spice mix, stir, reduce the heat and cook for two minutes.
4. Add the chickpeas, stir to coat all of the pieces and add the water.
5. Add half of the chilies and quinoa.
6. Serve garnished with chopped coriander leaves.
7. Your dish is ready to be served.

- **Wok Chili Paneer**

Preparation Time: 5 minutes

Cooking Time: 15 minutes

Serving: 4

Ingredients:

- Paneer cubes, two cups
- Corn flour, one tbsp.
- Salt, to taste
- Black pepper, as required
- Chilies, one tsp.
- Pepper, two tbsp.
- Soy sauce, one tbsp.
- Tomato sauce, two tbsp.

- Onion, two tbsp.

Instructions:

1. Mix the paneer cubes with corn flour, salt and pepper, fry it in a wok until the cubes brown.

2. In a wok fry the onions until brown, then add the chilies and cook for a couple of minutes.

3. Pop in the peppers and fry.

4. Add the paneer.

5. Now pour in the tomato and soy sauce.

6. Season and stir fry for five minutes.

7. Your dish is ready to be served.

- **Wok Hakka Noodles**

Preparation Time: 20 minutes

Cooking Time: 30 minutes

Serving: 4

Ingredients:

- Sesame oil, one tsp.
- Chili oil, one tsp.
- Spring onion, half cup
- Vinegar, one tsp.
- Soy sauce, one tbsp.
- Onion, one
- Capsicum, one
- Cabbage, one
- Carrot, one
- Garlic and ginger paste, one tbsp.

- Salt and pepper, to taste
- Green chilies, four

Instructions:

1. Heat sesame and chili oil in a wok.

2. Once the oil is hot, add garlic and ginger and fry.

3. Add onion, green chilies and white part of spring onion and fry.

4. Add carrot, capsicum and cabbage and fry.

5. Add soy sauce, vinegar, green chili sauce, salt and pepper and boiled noodles and toss nicely.

6. Cook for five minutes.

7. Garnish with spring onion greens.

8. Your dish is ready to be served.

- **Wok Indo Chinese Fried Rice**

Preparation Time: 5 minutes

Cooking Time: 30 minutes

Serving Size: 4

Ingredients:

- Fish sauce, two tbsp.
- Soy sauce, half cup
- Cooked brown rice, three cups
- Tomatoes, two
- Cilantro, half cup
- Salt and pepper, to taste
- Vegetable oil, two tbsp.
- Indian chili peppers, three

- Toasted walnuts, half cup
- Onion, one
- Scallions, half cup
- Minced garlic, one tsp.

Instructions:

1. Heat a large nonstick wok over high heat.
2. When the wok is very hot, add two tsp of the oil.
3. Add the remaining oil to the wok and add the onion, scallions and garlic.
4. Sauté for a minute, add the vegetables and chili pepper if using, tomatoes and stir in all the rice.
5. Add the soy sauce and fish sauce, stir to mix all the ingredients.
6. Adjust soy sauce if needed and stir well for another thirty seconds.
7. Your dish is ready to be served.

- **Wok Stir Fried Okra with Spices**

Preparation Time: 10 minutes

Cooking Time: 12 minutes

Serving: 4

Ingredients:

- Okra, two pounds
- Oil, half cup
- Onions, two cups
- Mixed Indian spice, two tsp.
- Tomatoes, two cups

- Chilies, three to four

Instructions:

1. Fry the okra in the oil and remove the okra once cooked.

2. Add the onions and let it brown.

3. Add the tomatoes and mixed spice.

4. Add the okras and chilies.

5. Let it cook for two minutes.

6. Your dish is ready to be served.

- **Wok Indian Seared Vegetables**

Preparation Time: 10 minutes

Cooking Time: 20 minutes

Serving: 2

Ingredients:

- Vegetable oil, half cup
- Ginger paste, one tsp.
- Mixed vegetables, one cup
- Garam masala, half tsp.
- Coriander powder, one tsp.
- Chili powder, one tbsp.
- Cardamom, six
- Garlic paste, one tsp.
- Yoghurt, one cup
- Salt, to taste
- Coriander, as required

- Onion, two
- Saffron, a pinch

Instructions:

1. Heat the vegetable oil into a pan.
2. Put cardamom, cloves, garlic and fry the mix properly.
3. Then add the vegetables and let it cook for about two minutes.
4. Add coriander and chili powder.
5. Add salt to taste.
6. Add ginger paste, mixture of fried onions and yogurt, let it cook for a minute.
7. Then put garam masala and saffron for flavor.
8. Cover it and give it some Time to cook on slow fire.
9. Let it cook for ten minutes.
10. Garnish it with coriander.
11. Your dish is ready to be served.

- **Wok Indian Stir-Fried Carrots**

Preparation Time: 10 minutes

Cooking Time: 5 minutes

Serving: 4

Ingredients:

- Soy sauce, two tbsp.
- Mixed pepper, two tbsp.
- Carrots, two cups
- Vegetable oil, two tbsp.
- Cornstarch, two tbsp.

- Indian mixed spice, one tsp.
- Pepper to taste
- Salt, as required

Instructions:

1. Add the oil in a wok.
2. Add in the carrots and cook it properly.
3. Add the carrots and rest of the ingredients.
4. In the end add the cornstarch and once the dish thickens, switch off the heat.
5. Your dish is ready to be served.

- **Wok Indian Five Spice Vegetarian Stir-Fry**

Preparation Time: 10 minutes

Cooking Time: 20 minutes

Serving: 4

Ingredients:

- Five spice mix, one tbsp.
- Garlic, one tsp.
- Oil, two tbsp.
- Mixed vegetables, two cups
- Sirarcha sauce, one tbsp.
- Fresh coriander, as required
- Salt, as required

Instructions:

1. Put two tablespoons of the oil into a wok.
2. When the oil is really hot, add all the vegetables except the garlic.

3. Add the garlic and fry until it is golden brown.

4. Add the Sriracha and fresh coriander to the vegetables and mix through.

5. Add the five-spice to the garlic and heat just for a few seconds.

6. Mix all the things, add salt and cook for five minutes.

7. Your dish is ready to be served.

Conclusion

Wok is an amazing kitchen utensil that has been used for many years in different cuisines. Indian, Chinese and Thai cooking is deeply influenced by wok cooking. In this book, we discussed the different recipes originated from the Thai, Chinese, and Indian cuisines that have been cooked using a wok.

We have discussed 77 different recipes comprising of breakfast, lunch, dinner, snack, and vegetarian recipes from the Chinese, Indian and Thai cousin using Wok for cooking. You can easily make all these recipes at home without any problem with the detailed ingredient list and easy to follow instructions. So, now you can cook easily the recipes of your choice, using a wok like a professional.

Printed in Great Britain
by Amazon

54243663R00058